Mother,

I Don't See Things
Like You Do!

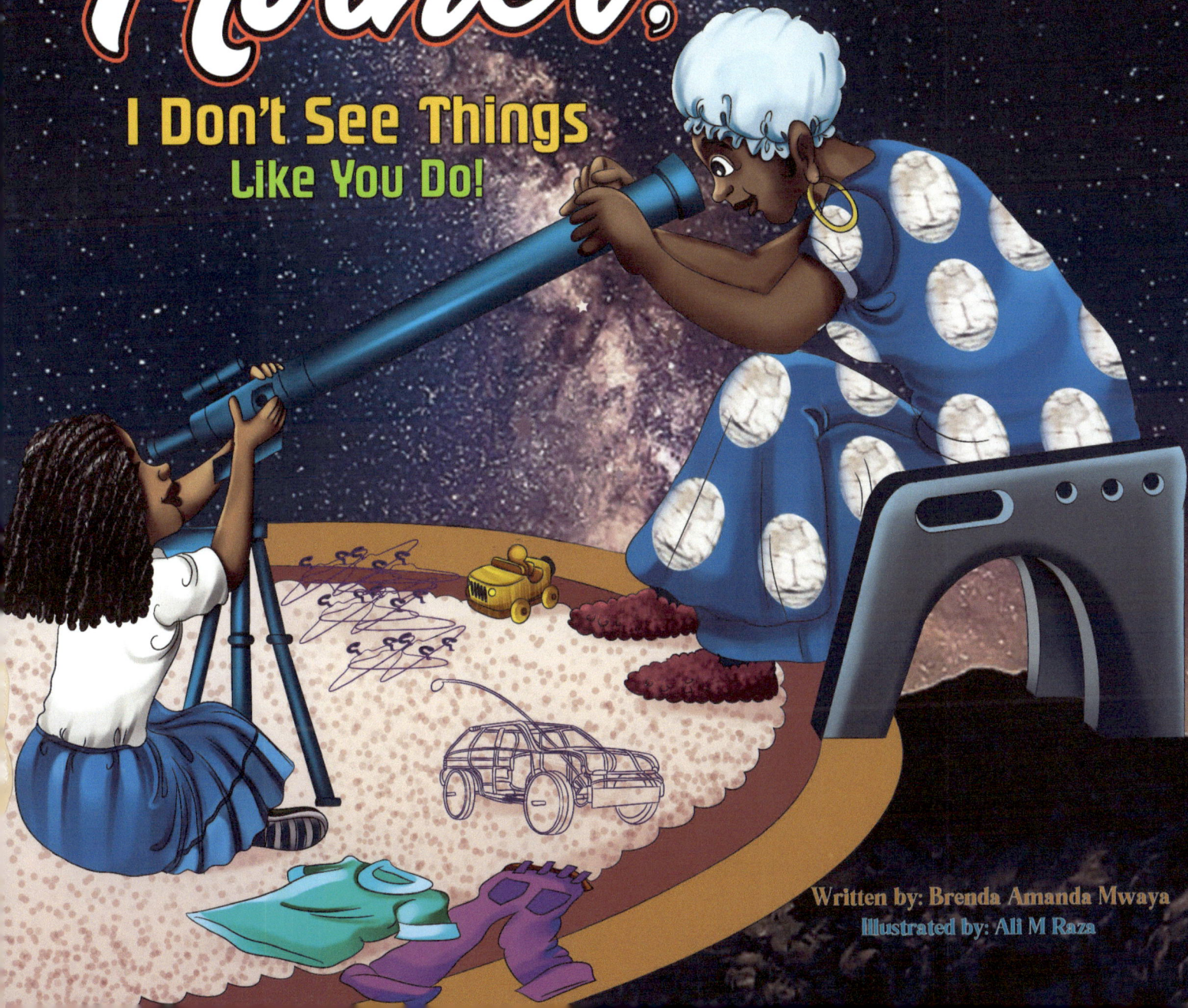

Written by: Brenda Amanda Mwaya

Illustrated by: Ali M Raza

1st Edition 2022

ISBN: 978-1-7334653-5-9 (Paperback)
ISBN: 978-1-7334653-6-6 (Ebook/Kindle)
ISBN: 978-1-7334653-7-3 (Hardback/Case)
ISBN: 978-1-7334653-8-0 (Spanish Edition)
ISBN: 978-1-7334653-9-7 (Coloring Book)

Library of Congress Control Number: 2022914226

Printed in the U.S.A.

DEDICATION

This children's book is dedicated to God, The One who prompted me to see the beauty in my daughter's imperfections alongside mine in our journey together. Ms. M.A.B. You were born a creator,designer, an artist and so many other beautiful things! Yet, I wanted to make a home-maker out of you! Roman, your creation made me see you clearly. You are an engineer and you are outstanding!

Ms.Bea Bair S., another little girl and personality that screams greatness. The world awaits the multi talents in you. Soar!

To every child out there who is already manifesting greatness, do not let anybody stop you. May your gifts receive real cultivation as you soar to change the world! You were born to positively mark the Earth like only you can!

To that guardian out there for that child, please pay attention. Avoid planting a fish in the soil. Let's get our future generation right. A musician born to do just that is so powerful and fulfilled making the world a better place for those that live in it. Should everyone become a doctor or an engineer? God forbid,then the rest of the world will be in trouble!

"Mooooom!" calls Marvell from her family's kitchen.

"Coming!" Mother answers as she runs down the stairs.

"What is it, Marvell?" asks her mother.

"Mother, where did all these dirty dishes come from?" Marvell unhappily asks.

"Why must I do all these dishes, Mother? Why must I even rinse the dishes before they go in the dishwasher? What is the purpose of the dishwasher, anyway!"

"And why do you insist on me doing some of the dishes by hand, like pots and pans? I can't do this. I don't want to do this! What is the purpose of doing the dishes anyway, Mother?"

"My child, some pots and pans do not wash very well in dishwashers. Besides, doing dishes by hand teaches you how to do this type of chore without the luxuries of a dishwasher. Not everywhere you go will have a dishwasher for cleaning dirty dishes,anyway. Not every person in the world depends on a dishwasher," Marvell's mother explains.

"Who cares about these stupid dishes anyway?" Marvell responds annoyedly.

"I do. One day you will too," Marvell's mother responds.

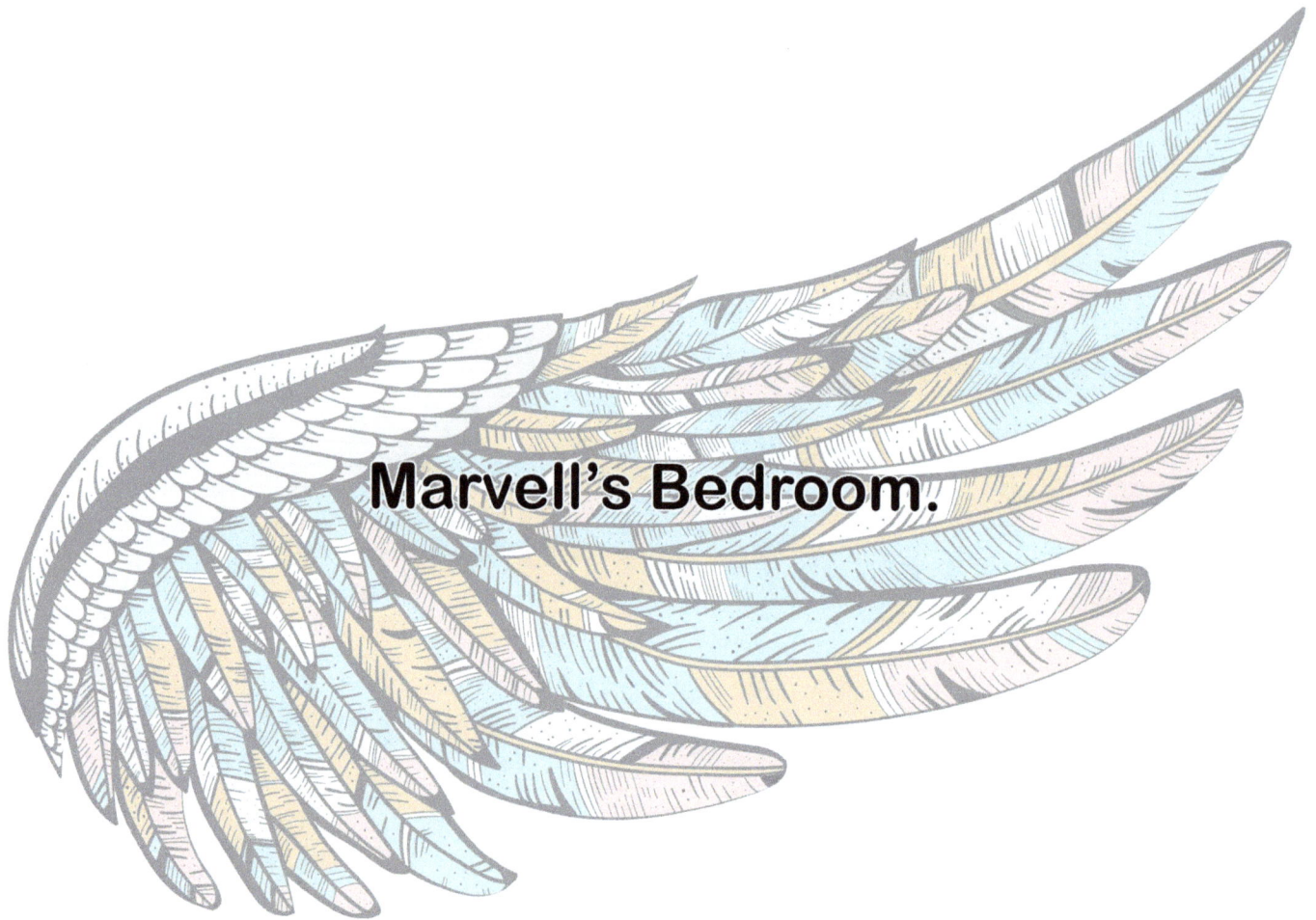

Marvell's Bedroom.

"Mooooom! I like my bedroom this way. Why should I make my bed every morning when I wake up? You know I have to lay back in there tonight,"complains Marvell.

"My child, is there enough space for you to lay on your bed tonight? Each night when you go to bed, you have all these clothes and so many things on top of your bed," beckons Mother.

"And why is everything such a debate?"

"Mother, I know where everything is in here. I can always find what I'm looking for when I need it. Why must I clean my bedroom?" pleads Marvell.

"Marvell, other people live in this house too. Whatever goes rotten in one part of the house can spread the smells to the rest of the house. Unattended food is bait for house rodents. So please clean the room," Mother annoyedly pleads.

"Mother, I don't want to waste quality time cleaning my room when I could be doing better things here," sighs Marvell.

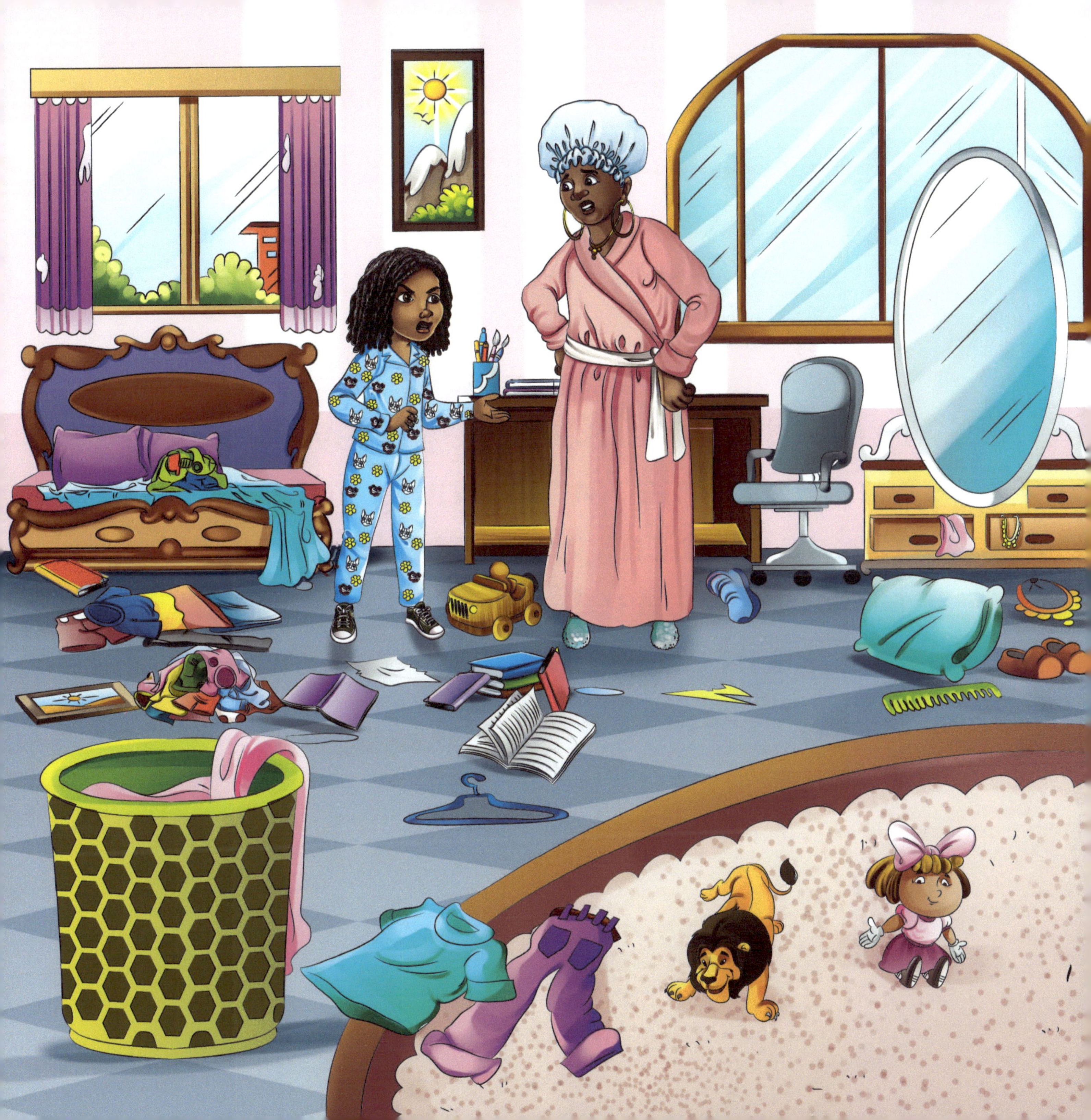

"My child, there is a time for everything each day. Time for cleaning your room is one of them. So clean this room already, please!" Marvell's mother spoke in an exasperated manner.

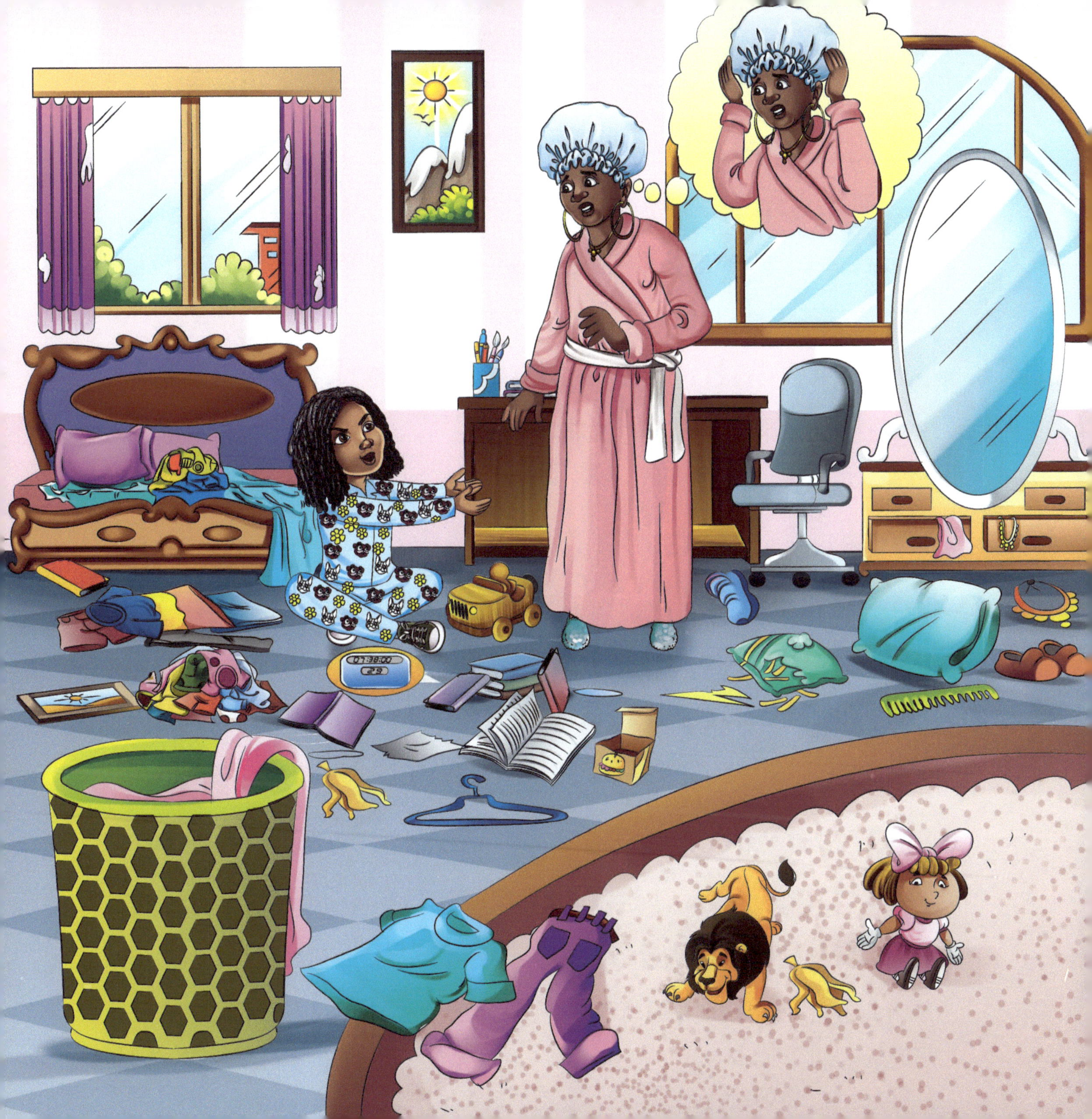
07:38:00
29

"Mother, look at this! My masterpiece. Don't you just love it? This is what I spent days in my room putting together! A car made out of wires from my wardrobe hangers. What do you think, Mother?" Marvell exclaims in elation, her face lit up. "Wow! This is awesome, my child! You have to build indeed. A day is not well balanced if one sits all day long building but forgets everything else all around one, though. There are important things we must do with others.

Personal chores are good for one's growth. They teach us to be accountable and to be responsible! I just want you to remember that."

"Mother, why must I come downstairs right now? I am not hungry!" Marvell declares. "Come downstairs at this very moment, Marvell!" Mother exclaims.

"Ok, Mother, here I come!" Marvell says gleefully.

"Mommy, Daddy, and little brother Daud, may I be excused from the dinner table, please?" pleads Marvell.

"Absolutely not! You just got here! You have hardly touched your food." Both parents almost spoke in unison.

"Mother, when will this dinner be over so that I can go back to my room?"

"Sweetheart, can you not spare a few moments with your family?

Please go to the living room and wait for us there in silence," Mother says discontentedly.

"Now we will never know what else I could have been building upstairs instead of sitting down here doing nothing on this couch," Marvell whines dejectedly underneath her breath.

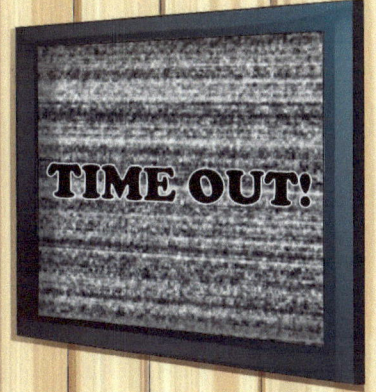

"Mother, may I speak with you? Please come," Marvell asks timidly. "Yes, my child, we can talk. Let's sit down, Marvell's mother agrees.

"Mother, I am sorry that I do not see things like you do. I do not mean to do things against you sometimes. It's just that doing dishes every now and again, keeping my bedroom spick and span all the time, and spending loads of time at the dinner table take up so much time. I would rather use that time for building gadgets and gizmos. That is exciting to me!"

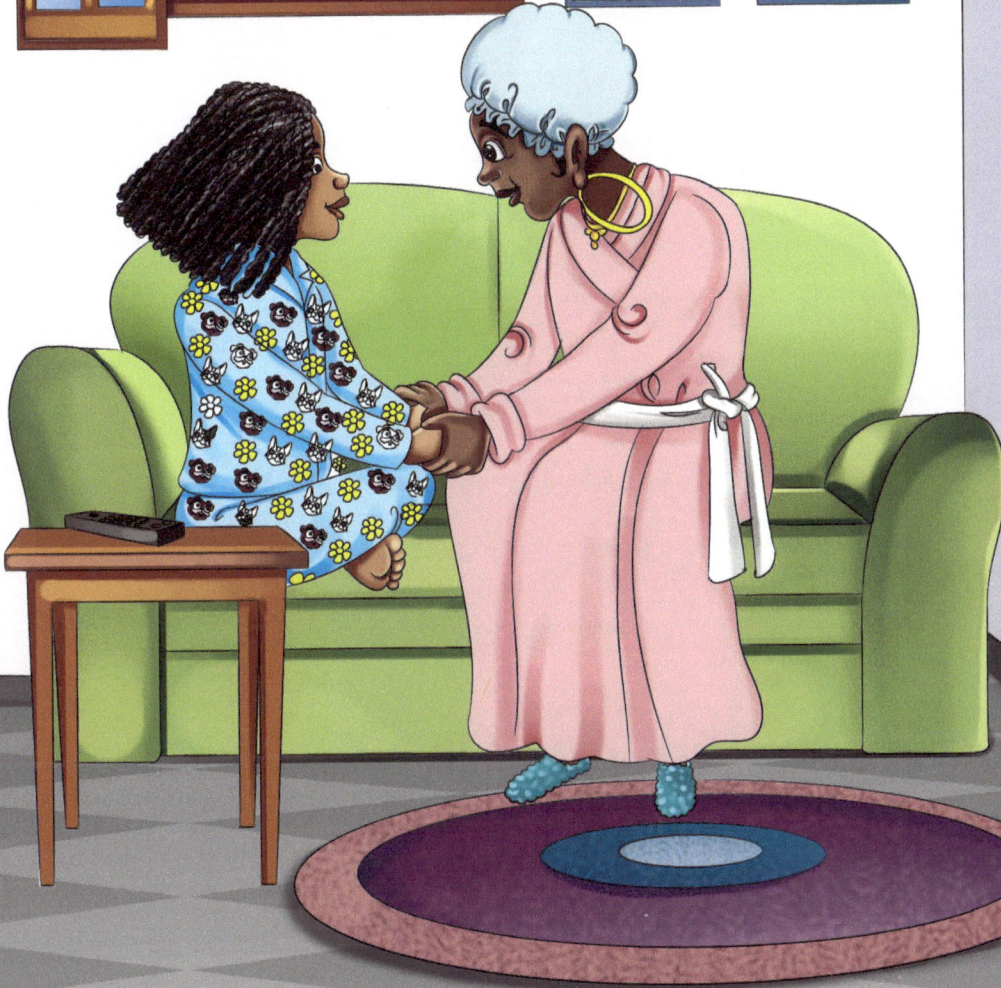

"My child, I wish you could see what I see. There is a world of responsibilities out there as you grow older. It all starts in your childhood by way of practice, by doing all these chores around the house. One day, you will thank me for teaching you some things around the house aside from your love of building gizmos," Mother explains lovingly.

"Mother, I love you so much!" Marvell exclaims.

"Sweetheart, I love you more!" cries Marvell's mother.

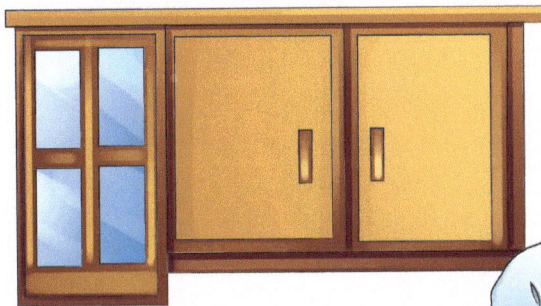

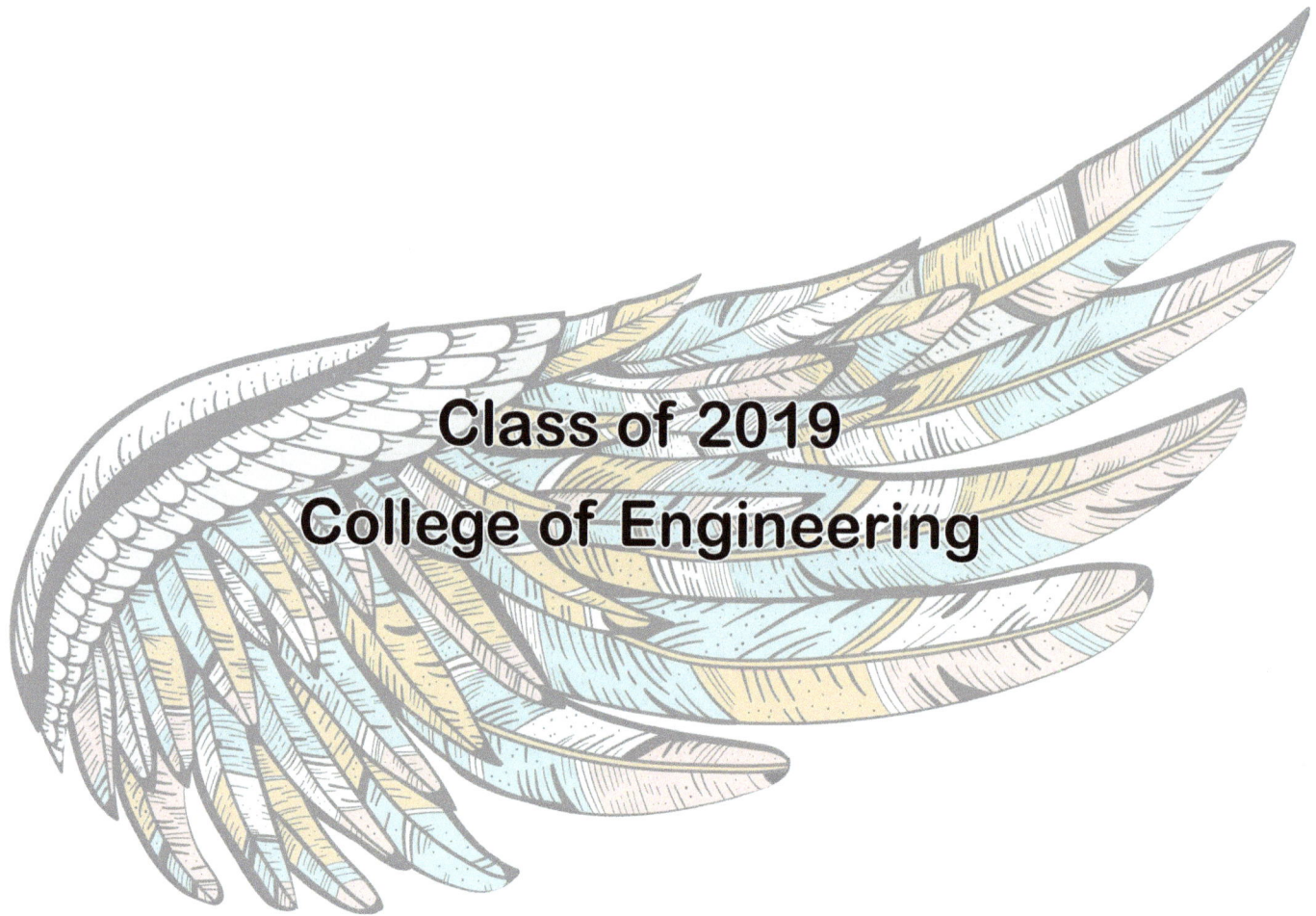

Class of 2019
College of Engineering

ABOUT THE ILLUSTRATOR

Ali M. Raza is a native of Pakistan. He is a graduate from Punjab University Lahore, Pakistan. He has been a professional children's book illustrator since 2018. He loves to play badminton, and loves to travel when he is not working. His greatest teacher is his father, who always reminds him that the only thing that matters in life is character, Nothing else.

ABOUT THE AUTHOR

Brenda Amanda Mwaya is a native of Malawi. A mother to four beautiful children. A designer, Inventor, a patent holder, a YouTuber and a fine cook who showcases her cooking on her YouTube channel titled "BrendasFood". She is also an author. In September of 2019, Brenda published her first non-fiction book titled "An Illegal Immigrant's Journey: How America Became My Destiny." In December of 2019, she published an illustrated children's book titled "If You Are A Kid Straight Out Of Philly". She is also a well seasoned professional nanny in Philadelphia.

www.ingramcontent.com/pod-product-compliance
Lightning Source LLC
Chambersburg PA
CBHW042011090426

42811CB00015B/1610